THIS BOOK

BELONGS TO

....

....

Thank you for Purchasing my book and taking the time to read it from front to back. I am always grateful when a reader chooses my work and I hope you enjoyed it!

With the vast selection available online, I am touched that you chose to be purchasing my work and take valuable time out of your life to read it. My hope is that you feel you made the right decision.

I very much would like to know what you thought of the book. Please take the time to write an honest and informative review on Amazon.com. Your experience and opinions will be of great benefit to me and those readers looking to make an informed choice.

With much thanks.

Table of Contents

SUMMARY

The Enchanting World of Crochet

Unveiling the Magic of Crochet

Crochet, a word derived from the Old French term 'crochet,' meaning 'small hook,' transcends mere stitching, enveloping crafters in a world where yarn and hook converge to breathe life into creations that mirror the artisan's creativity and finesse. The enchanting world of crochet encompasses a realm where each loop, stitch, and pattern interlaces not only fibers of yarn but also threads of cultural narratives, history, and individual expression.

A Tapestry of History

The history of crochet is as intricate as the patterns embedded in it. Although its origins remain somewhat elusive, the craft of crochet has interwoven itself through the fabric of various cultures and epochs. From the lace-like 'nun's work' of 17th-century nuns to the vibrant, resilient patterns crafted by Irish women during the potato famine, crochet has perpetually emerged as an art form that signifies both beauty and resilience. It has been a craft that has transcended socioeconomic boundaries, being cherished by both aristocrats and common folk alike for its utility and aesthetic charm.

A Global Stitch

Crochet has gracefully stitched its way across the globe, with each region infusing its own cultural, social, and artistic influences into the craft. From the delicate lacework that adorns European heirlooms to the vibrant, bold patterns found in South American tapestries, crochet serves as a canvas reflecting a tapestry of regional narratives, traditions, and aesthetic principles. It is a craft that has seamlessly melded functionality with artistry, providing a means through which artisans can express their creativity, tell their stories, and even sustain their livelihoods.

The Therapeutic Threads

Beyond its aesthetic and practical applications, crochet emerges as a sanctuary of tranquility and mindfulness. The rhythmic dance of the hook and yarn, the gradual manifestation of patterns, and the soft, gentle textures serve as a meditative medium, providing a respite from the tumult of everyday life. Many crafters have found solace in the gentle loops and swirls of their creations, discovering a space where they can unwind, express, and find a serene sense of accomplishment.

An Ever-Evolving Art Form

In the contemporary tapestry of art and craft, crochet has evolved, intertwining traditional techniques with modern expressions and applications. The age-old stitches are now employed to craft modern wearables, avant-garde art installations, and even practical, everyday items, reflecting the versatile, adaptive nature of the craft. Moreover, with the advent of technology, crochet has spun its web into the virtual world, where crafters from diverse corners of the globe converge, sharing patterns, techniques, and stories, thereby stitching a global community of crochet enthusiasts.

Conclusion

Embarking on a journey through the enchanting world of crochet is not merely about mastering a craft; it is about becoming a part of a rich, vibrant tapestry that spans across time and geography. It is about finding a medium through which one can express, connect, and find a serene sense of being. As we unravel the yarn and navigate through stitches and patterns, we weave our own narratives into a fabric that is perpetually evolving, perpetually creating. And thus, the enchanting world of crochet unfolds, inviting us to explore, create, and become a part of its timeless narrative.

Getting Acquainted with Tools and Materials

Embarking on your crochet journey entails familiarizing yourself with a myriad of tools and materials, each offering unique textures, sizes, and applications that can transform your crafting experience. Let's delve into the essentials to help you navigate through the vibrant world of crochet materials.

A. Understanding Crochet Hooks

Crochet hooks, the quintessential tool for any crocheter, come in various materials, sizes, and shapes, each providing a distinct crafting experience.

- **Materials**:

- **Metal Hooks**: Known for their durability and smooth surface, allowing yarn to glide effortlessly.

- **Wooden/Bamboo Hooks**: Celebrated for their lightweight and warmth, offering a comfortable grip and being gentle on the hands.

- **Plastic Hooks**: Lightweight and available in a multitude of sizes, especially larger dimensions.

- **Sizes**:

  - Hooks are available in numerous sizes, each suited for different yarn weights. The size of the hook affects the size of the stitches and the drape of the fabric.

  - Sizes may be denoted in millimeters (mm), letters (U.S.), or numbers (U.K. and Canada), thus, a conversion chart may be a handy reference.

- **Ergonomics**:

  - For those who crochet extensively, ergonomic hooks, designed to minimize hand and wrist strain, can be a worthy investment.

B. Yarn: A Tapestry of Textures and Colors

Yarn, the canvas upon which crochet creations come to life, is available in a spectrum of colors, fibers, and weights.

- **Types of Yarn**:

  - **Natural Fibers**: Include cotton, wool, alpaca, and silk, each providing a distinct texture and finish.

  - **Synthetic Fibers**: Such as acrylic and polyester, which are durable and often more budget-friendly.

  - **Blended Yarns**: Combine the properties of natural and synthetic fibers.

- **Yarn Weights**:

- Yarn weight refers to the thickness of the yarn strand, influencing the drape and appearance of the final piece. From lace-weight to super bulky yarn, each weight has its own charm and application.

- **Choosing the Right Yarn**:

  - The choice of yarn is pivotal, affecting the texture, appearance, and functionality of the crochet item. Consider the item's purpose, required care, and desired aesthetic when selecting yarn.

C. Additional Accessories

- **Stitch Markers**: Essential for marking specific stitches or rows, aiding in accurate and consistent crocheting.

- **Yarn Needles**: Used for weaving in ends and sewing together different crochet pieces.

- **Scissors**: A pair of sharp scissors is vital for cleanly cutting yarn.

- **Measuring Tape**: To ensure your projects are the desired size, especially crucial for wearable items.

D. Storing and Caring for Your Tools and Materials

- **Organizing Your Crochet Kit**: Keeping your tools and yarn organized not only makes it easier to find what you need but also protects materials from damage.

- **Caring for Yarn**: Understanding and following the care instructions of yarn (found on the yarn label) ensures longevity and maintains the quality of your crochet items.

Wrapping Up

Embarking on your crochet journey with a basic understanding of the tools and materials lays a strong foundation for a rewarding crafting experience. Your choice of hooks and yarn will evolve as you progress, discovering what textures, sizes, and materials resonate with your crafting style. So, allow yourself the freedom to explore, feel, and create with different materials as you weave through your crochet journey.

Crafting the Basic Stitches

Introduction to Crochet Stitches

Crochet, at its core, is about creating and combining a series of loops and knots using a crochet hook and yarn. These combinations, known as stitches, form the fabric of every crochet piece. Mastering these basic stitches is akin to learning the alphabet before writing sentences. They are the building blocks that, once learned, open a world of creativity and design.

Chain Stitch (ch): The Foundation

- **Purpose**: The chain stitch serves as the foundation for most crochet projects. It determines the width of the work and provides a base from which other stitches can be built.

- **Technique**:

    1. Start with a slip knot on the hook.

    2. Yarn over (wrap the yarn around the hook).

    3. Pull the yarn through the loop on the hook. This creates one chain stitch.

    4. Repeat the process to create a series of chain stitches.

- **Tips**: Maintaining consistent tension is vital. Too tight chains can make subsequent rows challenging to work into, while too loose chains can result in a wavy edge.

Single Crochet (sc): Compact and Firm

- **Purpose**: The single crochet stitch is one of the most fundamental stitches, creating a dense and firm fabric, ideal for projects that require a tighter weave, like dishcloths or amigurumi.

- **Technique**:

    1. Insert the hook into the desired stitch.

    2. Yarn over and pull up a loop. You will now have two loops on your hook.

3. Yarn over again and pull through both loops on the hook.

- **Tips**: Single crochet stitches are short, so ensure you're working into the correct part of your foundation chain or previous row to maintain evenness.

Double Crochet (dc): Versatile and Airy

- **Purpose**: Offering more height than the single crochet, the double crochet stitch provides flexibility to the fabric, making it suitable for scarves, blankets, and more.

- **Technique**:

  1. Yarn over and insert the hook into the desired stitch.

  2. Yarn over and pull up a loop. Three loops will now be on the hook.

  3. Yarn over and pull through the first two loops. Two loops remain.

  4. Yarn over again and pull through the remaining two loops.

- **Tips**: Due to its height, double crochet often results in a more 'holey' or lacy fabric. Combining it with other stitches can create interesting textures.

Exploring Consistency and Tension

- **Importance of Consistency**: Uniform stitches not only make the finished piece aesthetically pleasing but also ensure the structural integrity of the work.

- **Mastering Tension**: Tension refers to how tightly or loosely you hold the yarn while crocheting. It's a personal aspect of crochet, varying from one individual to another. The key is to find a comfortable tension that allows for consistent stitches.

Conclusion:

Mastering these basic stitches sets the foundation for an array of crochet projects. As one becomes proficient, they can combine these stitches, vary their sequence, and experiment with tension to discover a plethora of textures and patterns. With patience and practice, the beginner's initial stitches will evolve into a repertoire of crochet masterpieces.

Deciphering the Language of Crochet: Patterns and Symbols

Embarking on the crochet journey inevitably introduces crafters to the world of crochet patterns and symbols, a universal language that connects crocheters globally and acts as a blueprint for myriad creations. Mastering the art of reading patterns and understanding symbols opens up a vast realm of possibilities, enabling newbies to recreate intricate designs and eventually, craft their own.

Understanding Crochet Patterns

Crochet patterns serve as a guide, outlining the steps and techniques required to create a specific item. They are typically structured in a way that provides the crafter with all the necessary information, from materials to step-by-step instructions.

- **Materials List**: Identifies the type and amount of yarn, hook size, and any additional materials like buttons, stuffing, or beads.

- **Abbreviations and Terminologies**: Common crochet terms are abbreviated to streamline patterns. Some key abbreviations include:

    - ch: chain

    - sc: single crochet

    - dc: double crochet

    - sl st: slip stitch

    - st/sts: stitch/stitches

    - tog: together

- **Instructions**: Detailed guidelines that navigate through the creation process, often segmented into rows or rounds to facilitate clarity and trackability.

- **Notes and Tips**: Additional information or recommendations that may simplify complex steps or offer alternative approaches.

Diving into Symbols and Charts

Crochet charts and symbols are visual representations of patterns, providing a graphical guide that illustrates how a project evolves stitch by stitch. Charts can be particularly helpful in visualizing complex patterns and understanding the spatial relationships between stitches.

- **Basic Symbols**: Each stitch is represented by a unique symbol. For instance:
  - A small 'o' represents a chain.
  - An 'x' represents a single crochet.
  - A 'T' with a single hash represents a double crochet.

- **Reading Charts**: Charts are typically read from the bottom up. Right-handed crocheters will read from right to left on odd-numbered rows and left to right on even-numbered rows, while left-handed crocheters will do the opposite.

- **Repetitive Sections**: Often, patterns involve repeating a set of stitches multiple times, which is represented within a bracket or parentheses with a multiplier number or indicated by highlighting or shading on the chart.

Combining Patterns and Charts for Mastery

- **Simultaneous Usage**: Utilizing both written instructions and charts can enhance understanding, allowing the crafter to verify their work and ensure accuracy.

- **Practical Application**: Engage in simple projects that encourage the application of reading patterns and charts, solidifying learning through practical implementation.

Troubleshooting and Modifications

- **Identifying and Correcting Errors**: Acquire skills to spot discrepancies in your work compared to patterns and charts and learn techniques to amend them without having to unravel extensive work.

- **Making It Your Own**: As you become comfortable with patterns and charts, explore possibilities to modify and customize designs, infusing your unique touch into creations.

Conclusion

Mastering the language of crochet patterns and symbols not only empowers crafters to explore a diverse range of projects but also acts as a stepping stone towards becoming a creator of new designs. The ability to read, comprehend, and eventually, curate patterns, paves the way for boundless creativity, where every stitch contributes to a tapestry of personalized artistry.

From First Stitches to First Project: Embarking on the Crochet Journey

Commencing the Journey: Your First Stitches

Embarking on the journey of crochet begins with mastering the foundational stitches that will be the building blocks for all future projects. Learning and practicing these stitches will pave the way for a smooth and enjoyable crochet experience.

Chain Stitch: The Starting Point

- **Definition**: The chain stitch (abbreviated as "ch") forms the foundation of most crochet projects.

- **Technique**:

    - Create a slipknot and place it on the hook.

    - Yarn over (wrap the yarn over your hook) and pull it through the loop on the hook.

    - Repeat the process to create a series of chain stitches.

- **Application**: From forming the base of a project to creating spaces within patterns, the chain stitch's utility is vast and varied.

Single Crochet: Building Blocks of Your Fabric

- **Definition**: The single crochet stitch (abbreviated as "sc") is a compact stitch that creates a dense fabric.

- **Technique**:

    - Insert the hook into the desired stitch.

    - Yarn over and pull up a loop (you will have two loops on the hook).

    - Yarn over again and pull through both loops on the hook.

- **Application**: Ideal for projects that require a firm and solid fabric, such as potholders, bags, and amigurumi.

Crafting Your First Project: A Simple Dishcloth

A dishcloth is a quintessential first project for crochet beginners, providing a platform to apply and reinforce the stitches learned, without being overly complex or time-consuming.

Step 1: Gathering Materials

- **Yarn**: Opt for a cotton yarn, which is durable and washable, ideal for kitchen use.

- **Hook**: Choose a hook size that corresponds with your yarn (often recommended on the yarn label).

- **Additional Tools**: Scissors and a yarn needle to cut and weave in ends respectively.

Step 2: Creating the Foundation Chain

- Determine the width of the dishcloth (e.g., 8 inches).

- Make a slipknot and create a foundation chain of the length corresponding to the desired width. Remember that the width might slightly shrink or expand as you work, depending on your tension.

Step 3: Building the Fabric

- Work single crochet stitches across the foundation chain, creating the first row.

- To create subsequent rows, chain one (to turn) and work single crochet stitches across the previous row.

- Continue this process until the dishcloth reaches your desired length.

Step 4: Finishing Touches

- Once the desired size is achieved, cut the yarn, leaving a tail.

- Pull the tail through the last stitch, and use the yarn needle to weave in the ends securely.

Step 5: Revel in Your Achievement

Hold your finished dishcloth and revel in the accomplishment of transforming yarn into a tangible, usable object.

Reflections and Future Endeavors

- **Pondering Mistakes**: Mistakes and inconsistencies in your first project are not only common but also crucial for learning. Reflect on any challenges faced and explore solutions.

- **Experimentation**: Encourage experimenting with different yarns, colors, and stitch variations in future projects.

- **Progression**: Consider slightly complex projects for your next endeavor, perhaps introducing a new stitch or technique.

Embarking on this journey from learning stitches to completing a project, the progression from theory to practice brings about not only a sense of achievement but also a tangible product of your newfound skill. And remember: Every stitch counts, every row builds, and every project enhances your mastery in crochet.

Fixing Mistakes and Ensuring Consistency in Crochet

Embarking on your crochet journey is a delightful endeavor, but like all crafts, it comes with its unique set of challenges and hiccups. As a newbie, you'll inevitably encounter mistakes and inconsistencies in your work. This section dives deep into identifying, fixing common crochet mistakes, and maintaining consistency throughout your projects to ensure a smooth crafting experience.

Identifying Common Crochet Mistakes

- **Missed Stitches**: Sometimes, stitches might be skipped, leading to gaps and a decrease in stitch count.

- **Added Stitches**: Conversely, extra stitches might accidentally be added, altering the shape of the piece.

- **Inconsistent Stitch Size**: Variable tension can result in stitches of differing sizes, affecting the uniformity of the work.

- **Twisted Rows**: This occurs when the work is accidentally turned or twisted, disrupting the pattern and structure.

Tips for Preventing Mistakes

- **Count Your Stitches**: Regularly count stitches per row to ensure consistency and accuracy.

- **Use Stitch Markers**: Employ markers to indicate specific stitches or rows, acting as checkpoints.

- **Maintain Even Tension**: Practice maintaining consistent tension in your yarn to produce uniform stitches.

Fixing Mistakes with Grace

Crochet, fortunately, is a forgiving craft, allowing for corrections even after mistakes are made.

- **Undoing Stitches (Frogging)**: Learn how to carefully unravel stitches to return to a point before a mistake was made without damaging the yarn.

- **Correcting Missed or Added Stitches**: Understand techniques to discreetly add or decrease a stitch in subsequent rows to rectify errors without having to undo work.

- **Adjusting Tension**: Explore methods to subtly adjust tension in subsequent stitches to compensate for previous inconsistencies, ensuring the overall shape and size remain unaffected.

Techniques for Seamless Fixes

- **Invisible Increases/Decreases**: Implementing methods to add or remove stitches in a manner that is minimally noticeable in the overall pattern.

- **Hiding Yarn Ends**: Master techniques to weave in yarn ends securely, ensuring they remain hidden and do not unravel with use.

Ensuring Consistency in Crochet Projects

Maintaining a consistent rhythm and technique in crochet not only enhances the aesthetic appeal of the final product but also ensures its durability and shape.

- **Consistent Yarn Usage**: Stick to the same type and brand of yarn throughout a project to maintain uniform texture and color.

- **Uniform Stitching**: Employ a consistent technique for each stitch type to ensure the overall appearance remains cohesive.

- **Pattern Repeats**: Double-check pattern repeats and transitions to ensure they align perfectly and do not disrupt the flow of the design.

Practice and Mindfulness

- **Mindful Crocheting**: Engage in mindful crocheting, paying attention to each stitch, ensuring they are crafted with consistency and care.

- **Regular Review**: Periodically review your work, checking for any deviations or errors that might have crept in, allowing for timely corrections.

In the realm of crochet, mistakes are not setbacks but learning experiences, guiding you toward mastering the craft. Through understanding how to identify, fix, and prevent common crochet mistakes, and by ensuring consistency in your work, you pave the way for creations that are not only aesthetically pleasing but also crafted with precision and skill. This knowledge enables you to navigate through your crochet journey with confidence and poise, ensuring every stitch brings you closer to effortless crafting.

Advanced Techniques: Beyond the Basics

Embarking beyond the rudimentary stitches and elementary projects, this segment delves into advanced crochet techniques that unlock a myriad of possibilities in crafting diverse, intricate, and sophisticated creations.

Increasing and Decreasing Stitches

Understanding how to intentionally increase and decrease stitches is pivotal for shaping and tailoring crochet work to create a myriad of items, from wearables to decorative pieces.

- **Increasing**: This involves adding extra stitches to expand the work. It's crucial in crafting shapes like triangles or circles and creating wearables that require a specific fit. Various stitches (single, double, treble crochet, etc.) and methods to seamlessly integrate increases will be discussed, with a focus on maintaining a clean and even fabric.

- **Decreasing**: Conversely, decreasing stitches helps to taper and constrict the work. This technique is vital for crafting items like hats or amigurumi (crocheted stuffed toys). A detailed guide on how to decrease stitches without leaving gaps and maintaining a smooth texture will be outlined.

Practical tips, visual aids, and practice exercises will be provided to help readers master increasing and decreasing stitches with various types of stitches.

Working in the Round

Crocheting in the round opens avenues to create a plethora of items like coasters, hats, bags, and amigurumi. This section will introduce:

- **Magic Circle**: This technique is often used to start crocheting in the round, providing a tight, gapless center, which is especially crucial for items like beanies and amigurumi.

- **Joining Rounds vs. Spiral Crochet**: The distinction between joining rounds (closing each round with a slip stitch) and spiral crochet (working continuously without joining) will be detailed, exploring the applications and advantages of each method.

- **Shaping in the Round**: Techniques to achieve various shapes (e.g., cylinders, spheres, cones) by strategically increasing and decreasing stitches will be explored through easy-to-follow tutorials.

Colorwork Techniques

Introducing color to crochet work enhances its visual appeal and allows for creative expression.

- **Color Changes**: A guide to changing colors seamlessly without disrupting the pattern, and managing yarn to avoid tangling.

- **Tapestry Crochet**: This technique allows for the creation of intricate color patterns and designs within the crochet work, enabling the crafting of detailed images, motifs, and geometric patterns.

Textured Stitches

Exploring stitches that add texture and depth to the crochet work, enhancing its aesthetic and tactile appeal.

- **Bobble, Puff, and Popcorn Stitches**: These stitches create prominent, textured "bubbles" on the fabric, adding a three-dimensional aspect to the work. Detailed instructions and applications for each stitch will be provided.

- **Front and Back Post Stitches**: Techniques to create ribbing and textured patterns, commonly used in crafting wearables like hats and sweaters.

Filet Crochet

An introduction to filet crochet, a technique that uses a combination of open and filled mesh squares to create intricate designs and images, often used in crafting delicate items like doilies, table runners, and curtains.

Concluding Notes

In mastering these advanced techniques, crocheters equip themselves with the skills to craft complex, detailed, and refined projects, transcending beyond basic crochet capabilities. This section will encourage practice, exploration, and the creation of their unique patterns and designs, propelling them towards crochet mastery.

Each technique and concept will be elucidated with clear instructions, visual guides, and practical tips to ensure understanding and mastery, steering beginners confidently into the realm of advanced crocheting.

Crafting Wearables - A Step into Fashionable Creations

Embarking on the delightful journey of crochet not only furnishes your skillset but also your wardrobe! Crafting wearables allows you to personalize your attire, ensuring a unique and cozy style that's tailor-made for you. From the simplicity of scarves to the intricate beauty of sweaters, crocheted wearables offer a rich tapestry of options for every crafter.

Creating a Classic Crochet Beanie

Beanies are a staple in crochet wearables – they are stylish, versatile, and perfect for beginners stepping into crafting wearables.

Understanding the Design:

- **Shape and Size**: Exploring the standard shapes of beanies and understanding how to size them according to different age groups.

- **Texture and Style**: Discussing how different stitches impact the texture and style of the beanie.

Step-by-Step Project: Basic Beanie

- **Materials List**: Detailing the type of yarn, the size of the crochet hook, and any additional materials needed.

- **Pattern and Instructions**: Providing a beginner-friendly pattern, complete with clear instructions and visuals, guiding through each step from forming the first loop to completing the final stitch.

- **Finishing Touches**: Exploring options for customizing beanies, such as adding a pom-pom, embroidery, or applique elements.

Weaving a Warm and Stylish Scarf

Scarves are not just a protective accessory for chilly weather, but also a statement piece that can be personalized to reflect individual style.

Understanding the Design:

- **Length and Width**: Examining standard scarf dimensions and how altering them affects the style and functionality.

- **Patterns and Colorwork**: Introduction to basic colorwork techniques, such as stripes and grids, which can elevate the visual appeal of a simple scarf.

Step-by-Step Project: Striped Scarf

- **Materials List**: A curated list of essentials to ensure readers can easily gather what they need.

- **Pattern and Instructions**: A detailed, beginner-friendly pattern, supported by step-by-step instructions and visual aids, ensuring clarity and ease of understanding.

- **Edging and Fringing**: Demonstrating how to add a clean edge and optional fringes to enhance aesthetics and finishing.

Tips for Crafting Wearables

- **Choosing the Right Yarn**: The importance of selecting suitable yarn for wearables considering factors like comfort, warmth, and durability.

- **Gauge and Fitting**: Highlighting the significance of maintaining the correct gauge to ensure the wearable fits as intended.

- **Caring for Your Creations**: Tips on washing, storing, and maintaining crochet wearables to ensure they stay beautiful and durable.

Personalizing and Adapting Designs

- **Adaptability**: Encouraging readers to explore and adapt patterns, emphasizing that crochet is a flexible art and creativity is its core.

- **Personal Touch**: Introducing ideas to personalize projects, such as integrating initials, choosing personalized color schemes, or adding unique embellishments.

In crafting wearables, beginners not only produce something beautiful and practical but also embed a piece of their personality and style into their creations. This section of the article aims to nurture their skills, guiding them gently from understanding designs to crafting their own wearables, ensuring they are well-equipped and confident to experiment and create freely in their future crochet endeavors.

Joining the Global Crochet Community

Embarking on your crochet journey need not be a solitary endeavor. The global crochet community is a vibrant, welcoming space where enthusiasts—from beginners to seasoned crafters—come together to share, learn, and celebrate the art of crochet. Becoming part of this community not only enriches your skills and knowledge but also provides a platform to share your creations and experiences, fostering connections with like-minded individuals worldwide.

Online Platforms and Forums

1. **Social Media Groups:**

   - Engage with numerous crochet groups on platforms like Facebook, Instagram, and Pinterest, where members share their creations, patterns, and crochet experiences.

   - Participate in discussions, seek advice, and share your own experiences and creations to inspire and get inspired.

2. **Forums and Websites:**

   - Explore forums like Ravelry and Crochetville, where you can find patterns, join discussions, and connect with other crocheters.

- Visit websites and blogs dedicated to crochet, offering a plethora of free patterns, tutorials, and valuable tips to enhance your crochet journey.

3. **YouTube Channels:**

- Subscribe to channels offering crochet tutorials and pattern walkthroughs, providing visual aid to enhance your skills.

- Engage in the comments section, sharing your thoughts and asking questions, as many creators actively interact with their viewers.

Local Crochet Groups and Workshops

1. **Meetup Groups:**

- Find local crochet or crafting groups on platforms like Meetup, where you can join sessions to craft together, exchange ideas, and share knowledge.

- Consider starting your own local group if there isn't one nearby, bringing together individuals who share an interest in crochet.

2. **Workshops and Classes:**

- Explore workshops, classes, and courses offered by local craft stores, community centers, or online platforms.

- Engaging in classes not only enhances your skills but also provides an opportunity to meet fellow crocheters.

Crochet Events and Exhibitions

1. **Craft and Yarn Fairs:**

- Attend local or international craft fairs, such as the Knitting & Stitching Show or Vogue Knitting Live, which often feature crochet prominently.

- Explore stalls, participate in workshops, and witness the vast array of possibilities that crochet offers.

2. **Exhibitions:**

- Visit exhibitions showcasing artisanal crochet work, providing a source of inspiration and a glimpse into the artistic potential of crochet.

- Engage with artists and creators, discussing techniques, inspirations, and the stories behind their creations.

Charity and Community Projects

1. **Charity Crocheting:**

   - Participate in charity projects where crocheters create items for those in need, such as preemie hats, blankets, and scarves.

   - Explore organizations like Warm Up America or Crochet for Cancer, contributing to causes and making a positive impact through your craft.

2. **Community Projects:**

   - Engage in community yarn-bombing projects or local exhibitions, contributing your crochet work to beautify spaces or for communal use.

   - Participate in collaborative projects, creating larger pieces with fellow crocheters, fostering community spirit and collective creation.

Crochet-Alongs (CALs)

- Join CALs organized by online platforms or local groups, where participants crochet a particular pattern or project simultaneously, sharing progress and supporting each other.

- Engage in forums and discussions related to the CAL, sharing your experiences, challenges, and accomplishments, and enjoying the collective energy of crafting together.

Conclusion

Joining the global crochet community allows you to immerse yourself in a space that appreciates and celebrates the intricacies and beauty of crochet. It offers an environment of continuous learning, sharing, and connection, ensuring your crochet journey is ever-evolving, inspiring, and rewarding. From online forums to local groups, from engaging in CALs to participating in charity projects, every aspect of the community offers unique experiences and learning opportunities, ensuring your crochet journey is enriched with connections, inspirations, and shared joy in crafting.

Transforming Passion into Business

Embarking on a journey from intertwining yarns to intertwining passion with profession, transforming a crochet hobby into a thriving business is a dream that can materialize with strategic planning, dedication, and a touch of entrepreneurial spirit. This section unfolds the tapestry of turning your crochet crafting skills into a sustainable business, navigating through various avenues such as selling handmade items, designing patterns, and teaching crochet.

A. Crafting and Selling Handmade Items

- **Identifying Your Niche**: Understanding your strengths and interests in crochet to define a unique selling proposition. This might include specializing in baby wear, home décor, or fashionable accessories.

- **Pricing Your Work**: Developing a pricing strategy that accounts for materials, time, skills, and market rates, ensuring profitability without compromising attractiveness.

- **Platforms for Selling**: Exploring various online platforms like Etsy, Ravelry, and even creating your own website, to showcase and sell your creations to a global audience.

- **Marketing and Branding**: Building a brand around your creations, incorporating consistent branding elements, engaging product photography, and authentic storytelling to connect with customers.

B. Designing and Selling Crochet Patterns

- **Mastering Pattern Writing**: Ensuring proficiency in writing clear, accurate, and user-friendly crochet patterns that cater to various skill levels.

- **Photography and Diagrams**: Incorporating high-quality images and clear stitch diagrams to make your patterns visually appealing and easy to follow.

- **Publishing and Distributing Patterns**: Utilizing platforms like Etsy, Ravelry, or your own website to sell patterns, and considering publishing in crochet magazines or compilations.

- **Engaging with the Designer Community**: Collaborating with other designers, participating in design contests, and being active in online forums to build reputation and network.

C. Teaching Crochet

- **Determining Your Teaching Style**: Identifying whether you prefer conducting live workshops, creating online courses, or one-on-one teaching sessions.

- **Developing a Curriculum**: Crafting a structured, comprehensive, and engaging teaching plan that caters to various learning styles and levels.

- **Promoting Your Classes**: Utilizing social media, local community boards, and crafting forums to advertise your classes and attract students.

- **Continuous Learning**: Ensuring that you continue to enhance your own crochet skills and teaching methodologies to offer the best to your students.

D. Engaging with the Crochet Community

- **Participating in Events**: Joining crochet fairs, workshops, and exhibitions to showcase your work, network with other professionals, and stay updated with industry trends.

- **Collaborations**: Collaborating with other crafters, bloggers, and brands for mutual promotion and expanding your reach.

- **Giving Back**: Engaging in charitable activities, like crafting for a cause or conducting free workshops, to give back to the community and build a positive brand image.

E. Legal and Financial Considerations

- **Setting Up the Business**: Understanding the legalities of setting up a business, including registration, taxation, and compliance.

- **Managing Finances**: Keeping meticulous records of income, expenses, investments, and understanding the financial health and sustainability of your business.

- **Protecting Your Work**: Learning about and securing intellectual property rights for your designs, patterns, and creations to safeguard against infringement.

Conclusion

Transforming a crochet hobby into a business requires intertwining crafting skills with business acumen. While the threads of creativity and passion are central, a structured business plan, customer engagement, and continuous learning and adaptation are the stitches that will shape your crochet business tapestry. A mindful blend of creativity, strategy, and engagement with the crochet community will pave the way for a successful and fulfilling crochet business journey.

Mindful Crocheting: An Intertwine of Tranquility and Creativity

Mindful Crocheting: A Symbiotic Relationship

The rhythmic, repetitive motion of crocheting, coupled with the soft touch of yarn and the gradual emergence of a crafted piece, inherently embeds mindfulness and tranquility into the practice. Mindful crocheting not only involves being present during the crafting process but also evokes a serene escapade that transcends beyond the physical act of creating stitches.

A. The Meditative Aspect of Crocheting

- **1. Stitching into Serenity**: Engaging in crochet often draws parallels with meditative practices, where the continuous looping and counting of stitches create a state of focused relaxation, allowing crafters to disengage from stress and anxiety.

- **2. Psychological and Emotional Well-being**: Numerous studies have highlighted the positive impact of engaging in crafts like crochet on mental health, offering a creative outlet that fosters self-expression, accomplishment, and emotional respite.

- **3. The Flow State**: Crocheting often leads to experiencing a 'flow state', where the crafter becomes deeply engrossed, losing track of time and external worries, and solely immersing in the joy of creating.

B. Sustainable Crafting: A Conscious Approach

- **1. Ethical Yarn Choices**: Adopting the use of eco-friendly yarns such as organic cotton, bamboo, or recycled materials reflects a mindful approach towards environmental impact. This section would explore various sustainable yarn options and where to source them.

- **2. Supporting Local and Ethical Businesses**: Choosing to purchase materials from local artisans or businesses that adhere to ethical practices not only ensures quality in your crafting endeavors but also supports sustainable practices within the industry.

- **3. Mindful Consumerism**: Encouraging crafters to be conscious of their consumption patterns, reducing waste, and valuing each crafted piece's time and resources.

C. Crochet as a Form of Self-care

- **1. Crafting Your Calm**: Allocating time for crocheting can be viewed as an act of self-care, providing a designated moment to unwind, create, and be with oneself amidst the hustle of daily life.

- **2. Celebrating Each Stitch**: Embracing every stitch and every project as a reflection of dedication, learning, and personal expression, and celebrating the imperfections and unique quirks they bring.

- **3. Crafting and Connecting**: While crocheting offers solitary peace, it can also form bonds when shared with a community. Engaging in crochet circles or online forums can create connections and offer shared joy in crafting together.

D. Mindfulness in Learning and Creating

- **1. Embracing Challenges with Patience**: Learning new stitches or tackling a complex pattern can be intricate. Approaching these challenges with patience and curiosity embodies the mindfulness that crocheting inherently brings.

- **2. The Joy in Creating**: Encouraging crafters to find joy in the process of creating, detaching from the pursuit of perfection, and immersing in the journey of bringing yarn to life.

E. Conclusion: Stitching Mindfulness into Daily Life

Embracing crocheting as a mindful practice intertwines creativity, tranquility, and conscious living into one's lifestyle. It stitches together moments of peace, instances of joy in creation, and a thoughtful approach towards crafting and consuming. As each loop and stitch forms, it not only crafts a tangible piece but also weaves a tapestry of mindful moments, gentle tranquility, and thoughtful crafting into the fabric of daily life.

This section will blend personal anecdotes, practical tips, and inspiring visuals to immerse the reader into the serene and mindful world of crocheting, encouraging them to stitch tranquility into their crafting journey.

Conclusion and Future Journey: Crafting Ahead with Confidence

A Recapitulation: The Journey So Far

Embarking on this expedition through the serene and intricate world of crochet, we traversed from understanding its historical and cultural significance to getting hands-on with the craft itself. We've woven through the essentials of crochet tools and materials, mastered the fundamental stitches, deciphered the language of patterns and charts, and even breathed life into yarn, transforming it into tangible items like dishcloths, beanies, and scarves.

Beyond the Basics: Infinite Possibilities Await

Crochet is not merely a craft; it's a universe of infinite creative possibilities, waiting to be explored and adored. The skills and knowledge accumulated through this initial journey lay a firm foundation, upon which myriad structures of creativity can be built. Advanced stitches, intricate patterns, and sophisticated projects like amigurumi, lacework, and garment-making await, ready to be explored and mastered in due time.

The Continuum of Learning: Embrace the Evolving Craft

Crochet, while rooted in tradition, continually evolves, intertwining with contemporary styles, techniques, and materials. The learning curve extends infinitely, with every project, pattern, and stitch revealing novel experiences and learnings. Online platforms, books, workshops, and crochet communities serve as boundless reservoirs of knowledge, ready to be tapped into and explored. New stitches, techniques, and patterns are continually emerging, offering fresh and exciting avenues to stroll through and discover.

Joining the Global Tapestry: Engaging with the Crochet Community

A vibrant and welcoming community of crafters across the globe awaits, ready to share, inspire, and be inspired. Engaging with this community through forums, social media platforms, and events allows for the exchange of ideas, knowledge, and inspiration, thereby enriching one's crochet journey manifold. Participate, share your creations, stories, and experiences, and let the threads of camaraderie weave through, creating a global tapestry of connected crafters.

Crafting for a Cause: Crochet with Purpose

Crochet can also become a medium through which positive change is woven into the society and environment. Engage in crafting for charitable causes, create products that speak for a cause, and adopt sustainable and ethical practices in choosing materials and projects. Your craft can become a voice, a helping hand, and a step towards positive change, intertwining creativity with responsibility and impact.

Transforming Passion into Livelihood: The Business of Crochet

For those who find their heart and soul entwined with the yarn, transforming this passion into a livelihood can be a fulfilling journey. From selling handcrafted items and designing patterns to teaching and blogging about crochet, numerous avenues can turn this serene hobby into a thriving business. Your unique style, creations, and journey can inspire and serve others in their crochet endeavors, weaving together a career that's crafted with passion and served with love.

Final Reflections: Cherishing Every Stitch

As we cast a glance back at the journey and peek into the future, let's embrace and cherish every stitch, every loop, and every project, for they are not just threads and knots but expressions of creativity, patience, and passion. May every stitch be a meditation, every pattern be an adventure, and every project be a story, crafting not just with yarn and hook but with heart and soul.

Resources for the Continued Journey

- **Further Reading**: Books and articles that explore advanced techniques, patterns, and projects.

- **Online Platforms**: Websites, forums, and social media groups that offer a space to learn, share, and engage.

- **Workshops and Events**: Information on upcoming workshops, webinars, and events that can enhance your skills and knowledge.

Closing Note

Here's sending forth a skein of gratitude, inspiration, and best wishes as you continue to explore, create, and cherish your journey through the enchanting world of crochet. May your hooks always dance, your yarn forever bring joy, and your creations always wrap you in warmth and satisfaction.

The journey does not end here; it simply transforms into a path that you now weave, stitch by beautiful stitch, into a tapestry that is uniquely, wonderfully yours. May your crochet adventures be ever vibrant, ever rewarding, and ever beautiful.

INTRODUCTION

You've finally done it; you've decided to expand your skill set in the creative world of crochet, welcome. Through these pages, you will learn step by step how to complete beautiful crochet stitches. To help with the process detailed photos are included for most stitches, making it even easier for you to learn. Along with stitches you will be introduced to crochet techniques encountered in countless patterns. This is a quick resource to help you enjoy, create, and conquer your next crochet pattern. Now if you are ready, let's start creating.

CHAIN STITCH

-Start by attaching a slip knot to your crochet hook.

-Hold your crochet hook in your right hand and hold the length of yarn in your left hand:

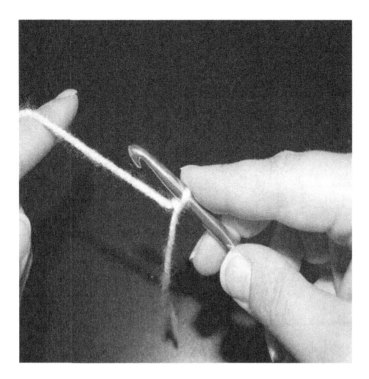

-Hold the slip knot end of your yarn for extra stability, then bring the yarn over in front of the hook.

-The yarn will come from back to front.

-With the yarn brought over the front of the hook, the yarn should rest in the throat of the hook:

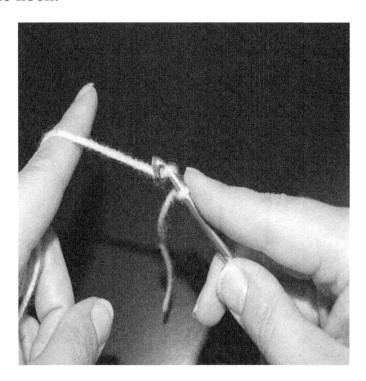

-Now gently pull the yarn crossed over the hook through the loop created by the starting slip knot.

-You've now completed your first chain stitch:

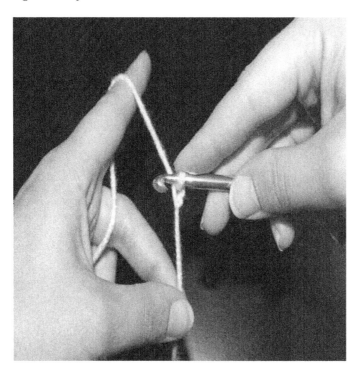

Tip: When counting a specific number of chain stitches for a pattern, do not count the slip knot.

SINGLE CROCHET STITCH

-Start with a foundation chain:

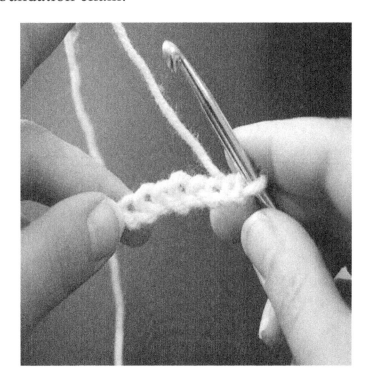

-Insert the crochet hook into the second chain stitch from the hook:

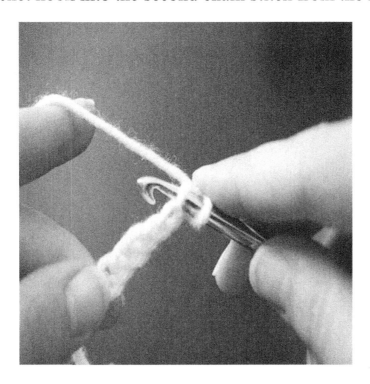

-Bring yarn over the crochet hook and gently pull through the chain (You will have 2 loops on the hook):

-Bring yarn over the crochet hook again and gently pull through both loops on the crochet hook.

-You've now completed your first single crochet:

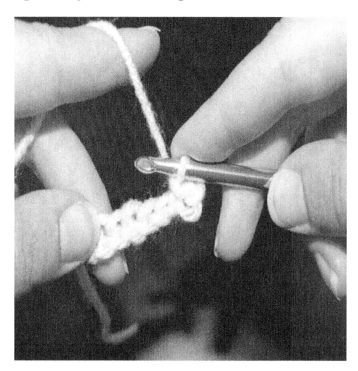

SLIP STITCH

-Start with a foundation chain:

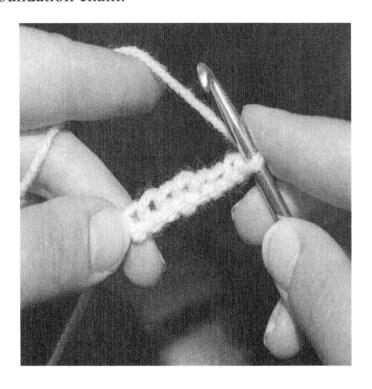

-Insert the crochet hook into the 2nd stitch from the hook:

-Now yarn over the crochet hook:

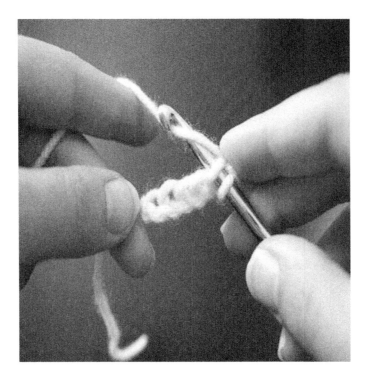

-Gently pull through the stitch and the loop on the crochet hook. You've completed your first slip stitch:

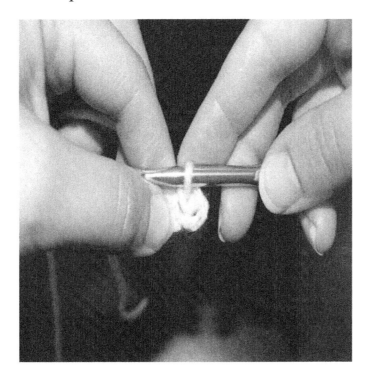

BUNDLE STITCH

-Start with a foundation chain:

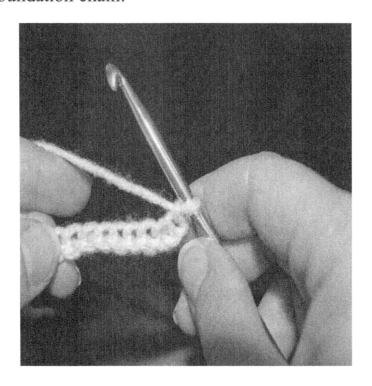

-Yarn over 1 time:

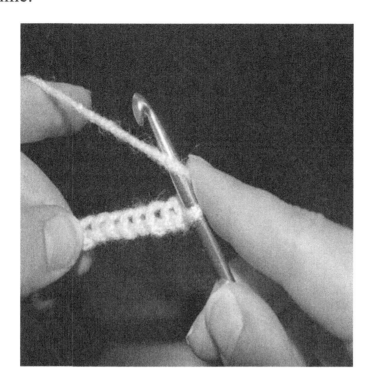

-Inset the crochet hook into the stitch and then yarn over 1 time:

-Gently pull crochet hook through the stitch.

-You will now repeat this process into the same stitch as many times as requested in a pattern:

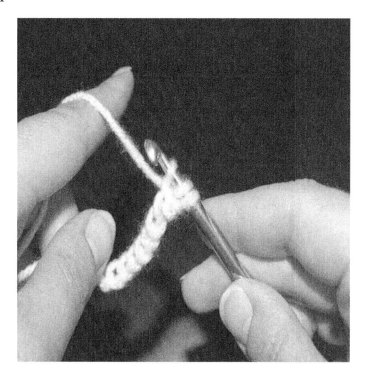

-To finish a bundle stitch, simply yarn over and gently pull through all loops on the crochet hook. Then chain 1. You've now completed your first bundle stitch:

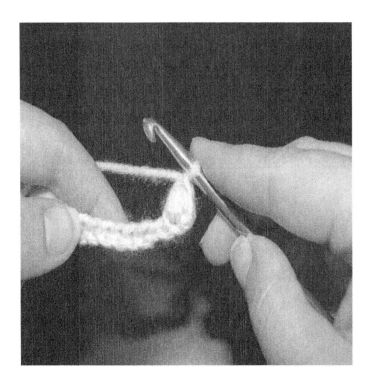

DOUBLE CROCHET STITCH

-Start with a foundation chain:

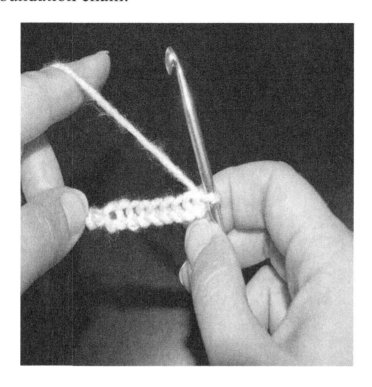

-Bring yarn over crochet hook and insert hook into the 4th chain from the crochet hook. Yarn over again and gently pull through (You will have 3 loops on your crochet hook):

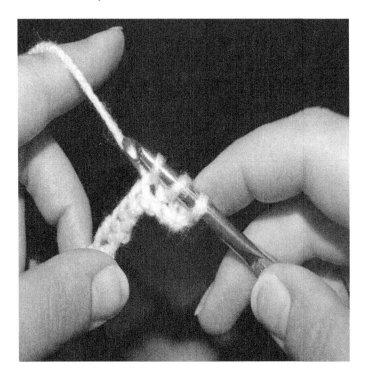

-Yarn over and then gently pull through first 2 loops on the crochet hook:

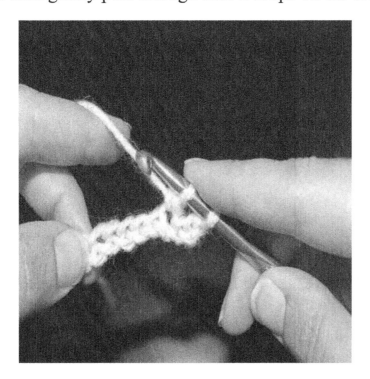

-Yarn over again and gently pull through the last 2 loops on the crochet hook. You've now completed your first double crochet:

DOUBLE TREBLE CROCHET STITCH

-Start with a foundation chain:

-Yarn over 3 times:

-Insert the crochet hook in the 6th stitch from the hook, then yarn over the crochet hook:

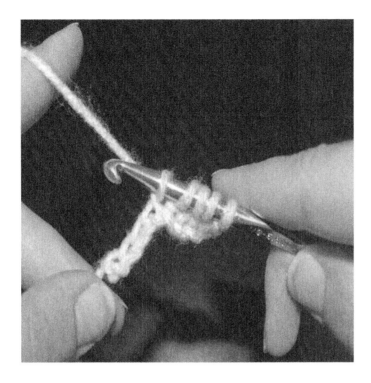

-Gently pull through the stitch:

-Yarn over:

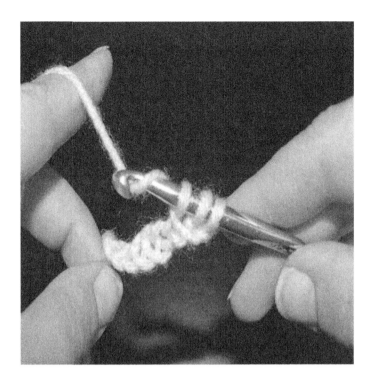

-Gently pull through the first 2 loops on the crochet hook, and then yarn over:

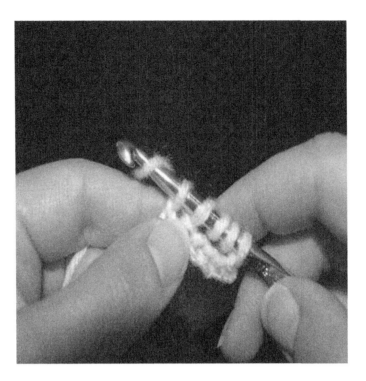

-Gently pull through the first 2 loops on the crochet hook, and then yarn over:

-Gently pull through the first 2 loops on the crochet hook, and then yarn over.

-Gradually pull through the final 2 loops on the crochet hook. You've completed your first double treble crochet stitch:

Tip: When completing a row of these, chain 5 and then turn.

HALF DOUBLE CROCHET STITCH

-Start with a foundation chain:

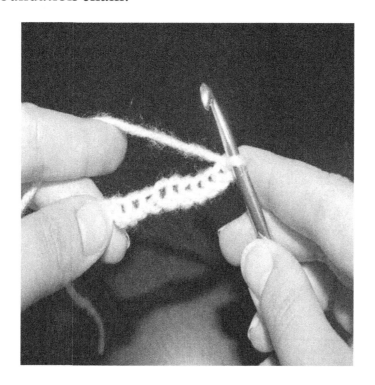

-Yarn over the crochet hook:

-Insert the crochet hook into the 3rd stitch from the hook:

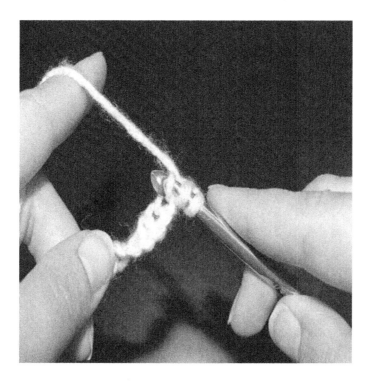

-Yarn over the crochet hook:

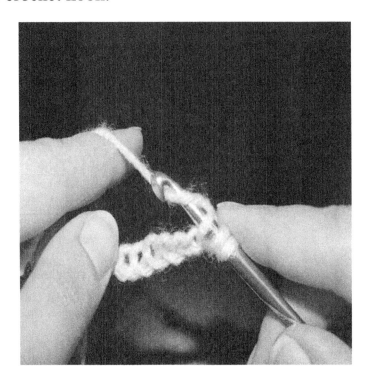

-Gently pull through the stitch:

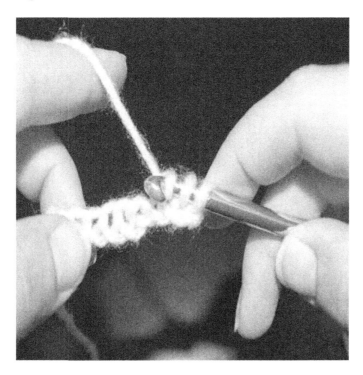

-Yarn over the crochet hook:

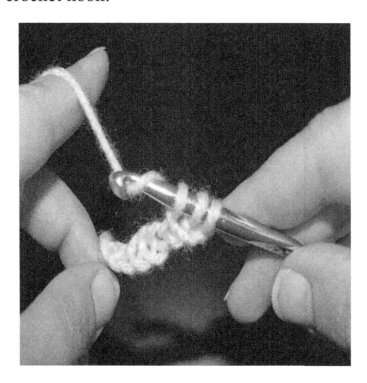

-Gently pull through all 3 of the loops on the crochet hook. You've completed your first half double crochet stitch:

Tip: When completing a row, you will need to chain 2 before turning your work.

HORIZONTAL RIBBING STITCH

-Start with a foundation chain:

-Insert the crochet hook underneath one strand of the top stitch:

-Work your desired stitch (for this example I used a double crochet stitch):

Tip: The strand not being used is what caused the horizontal bar appearance.

POPCORN STITCH

-Start with a foundation chain:

-Double crochet 4 or 5 double crochet into the stitch:

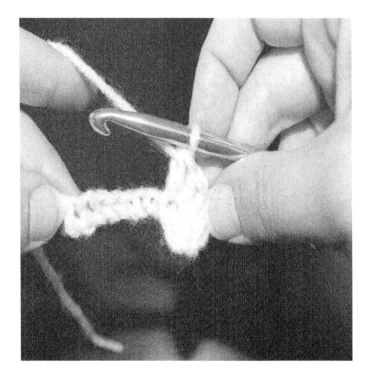

-Now remove the crochet hook from the loop and insert it into the first double crochet. The hook will go from front to back. Then pick up the loop you took off the crochet hook and gently pull it through. You've now completed your first popcorn stitch.

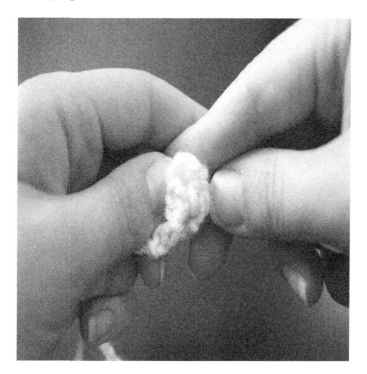

Tip: These directions will give the bumped texture on the front of your work. To achieve this appearance in the back of your work, simply insert your hook into the first double crochet from back to front.

PUFF STITCH

-Start with a foundation chain:

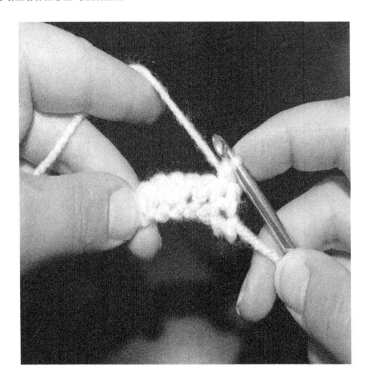

-Yarn over and insert the crochet hook into the specified stitch. Yarn over again and gently pull through the stitch:

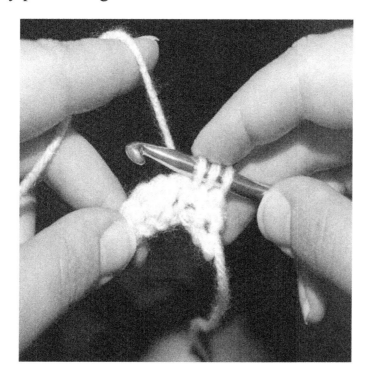

-Yarn over and insert the crochet hook into the specified stitch. Yarn over again and gently pull through the stitch (5 loops on the crochet hook):

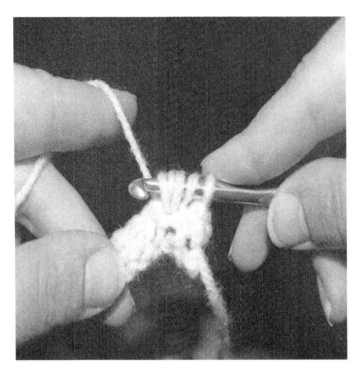

-Yarn over and insert the crochet hook into the specified stitch. Yarn over again and gently pull through the stitch (7 loops on the crochet hook):

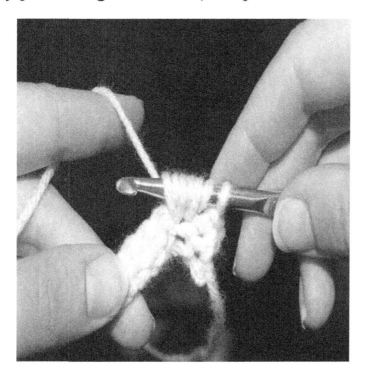

-Yarn over and gently pull through each of the 7 loops on the crochet hook. Then chain 1 to complete your first puff stitch:

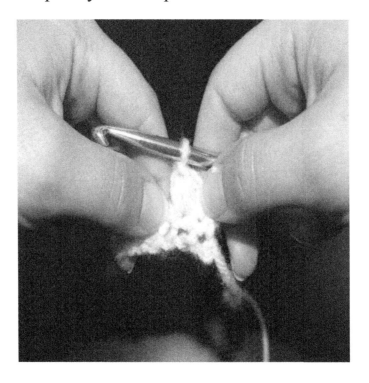

Tip: Your pattern will determine the number of loops on the hook when you complete your puff stitch. This was an example using 7 loops. Make sure to pay attention to what your pattern requires.

RAISED DOUBLE CROCHET STITCH (FRONT)

-Start with a foundation chain:

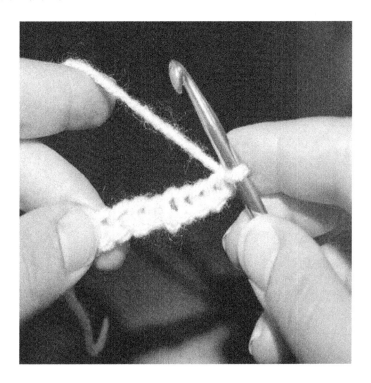

-First you will yarn over, and then insert the crochet hook from front to back and from right to left. This will be worked around the vertical strands of the stitch within the preceding row of stitches.

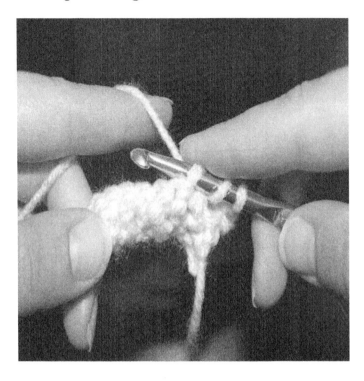

-Yarn over and gently pull through 2 loops. Yarn over and gently pull through 2 loops. You've completed your first raised double crochet stitch (front):

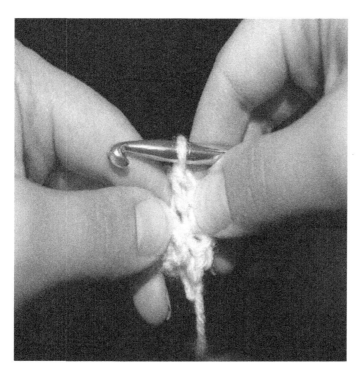

RAISED DOUBLE CROCHET STITCH (BACK)

-Start with a foundation chain:

-First you will yarn over, and then insert the crochet hook from back to front and from right to left. This will be worked around the vertical strands of the stitch within the preceding row of stitches:

-Yarn over and gently pull through 2 loops. Yarn over and gently pull through 2 loops. You've completed your first raised double crochet stitch (back):

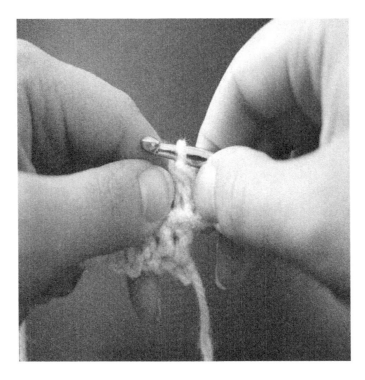

CRAB STITCH

-Start on a complete row. (Do not turn your work):

-Starting one stitch to the right insert the crochet hook from front to back.

-The crochet hook needs to be hook end facing down, then yarn over and gently pull through the proceeding row:

-Now yarn over:

-Gently pull through all of the loops on the crochet hook.

-Moving forward insert your hook in the next stitch and continue

Tip: This stitch is often used to decorate the edge of a piece or as reinforcement.

SHELL STITCH

-Start with a foundation chain.

-Skip the number of stitches required in your pattern.

-Insert the crochet hook into the next stitch.

-Complete 1 double crochet.

-Now continue to complete the number of double crochets required for your pattern.

-Skip the number of stitches you did before and repeat the previous step until all identical shell stitches are completed.

PICOT STITCH

-Start with a foundation chain.

-Chain 3.

-Single crochet into the 3rd chain stitch. You've completed your first picot stitch.

-Note: Your pattern will determine the number of chain stitches required for each picot stitch.

CROSSED DOUBLE CROCHET STITCH

-Start with a foundation chain.

-Yarn over 2 times and insert the crochet hook into the stitch in the preceding row.

-Gently pull through stitch. Yarn over and gently pull through 2 loops. (3 loops remaining on the crochet hook)

-Yarn over and then skip a stitch, inserting crochet hook the following stitch.

-Now yarn over and gently pull through the stitch. Yarn over and gently pull through 2 loops.

-Yarn over and gently pull through 2 (3 loops remaining on crochet hook).

-Yarn over pull through 2 loops. Yarn over pull through 2 loops. (1 loop remaining)

-Chain 1, yarn over, and insert the crochet hook underneath the upper strands of yarn where the preceding double crochet makes a cross.

-Gently pull through the stitch. Yarn over and gently pull through 2 loops. Yarn over pull through 2 loops. You've now completed your first crossed double crochet.

CROCHET PATTERNS

HOW TO READ A CROCHET PATTERN

When you start reading crochet patterns, especially ones that advance in difficulty it is easy to become confused. Following these helpful tips on reading crochet patterns, you will find a Crochet Pattern Abbreviation guide, which provides a quick resource for just about all symbols and shorthand you will encounter while working through a crochet pattern. Let's get started.

EXAMPLE PATTERN:

-Ch 30

-Row 1: Work 1 hdc in third chain from hook and in each ch across.

-Row 2: Ch 1 and turn. Work 1 hdc in each hdc in BACK LOOP only.

-Repeat row 2 until panel measure 6" from the beginning.

-Fasten off and leave a 12" tail.

EXAMPLE PATTERN (WITH EXPLANATION):

-Ch 30

So you will make 30 chains

-Row 1: Work 1 hdc in third chain from hook and in each ch across.

So start with the third chain from the hook you are going to half double crochet the entire row.

-Row 2: Ch 1 and turn. Work 1 hdc in each hdc in BACK LOOP only.

Chain 1 and then turn your work. Then using only the back loop half double crochet into each of the previous rows half double crochet.

-Repeat row 2 until panel measure 6" from the beginning.

Pretty easy to understand right, simply look back up to row 2 and repeat.

-Fasten off and leave a 12" tail.

Fasten off the yarn, but make sure to measure an extra 12" before cutting your yarn.

Crocheting patterns are not difficult if you understand that they are directions written in shorthand. Use the abbreviation guide to help you and don't hesitate to take notes on the pattern to help you along. Other things you will find on your pattern are: yarn weight suggestions and required crochet hook size.

CROCHET PATTERN ABBREVIATIONS

Below you will find abbreviations commonly found in crochet patterns. For easy reference they are listed in alphabetical order.

alt - alternate

approx - approximately

beg - beginning

bet - between

BL - back Loop, block

bo - bobble

BP - back post

BPdc - back post double crochet

BPsc - back post single crochet

BPtr - back post treble crochet

CA - color A

CB - color B

CC - contrasting color

ch - chain

chs - chains

CL - cluster

dc - double crochet

dc2tog - double crochet 2 stitches together

dec - decrease

dtr - double treble crochet

FL - front loop

FO - finished object

FP - front post

FPdc - front post double crochet

FPsc - front post single crochet

FPtr - front post treble crochet

g - gram

half dc or hdc - half double crochet

inc - increase

incl - include

m - meter

MC - main color

oz - ounce(s)

p - picot

pat - pattern

PM - place marker or place a marker

pc - popcorn

rep - repeat

rnd - round

rnds - rounds

sc - single crochet

sc2tog - single crochet 2 together

sk - skip

SL st - slip stitch

sp - space

sps - spaces

st - stitch

sts - stitches

tch - turning chain

tog - together

tr - treble crochet or triple crochet

tr tr - triple treble crochet

yo - yarn over

* - Repeat the directions with the asterisks as directed. This may be from another set of directions.

( ) - Complete work specified in parentheses the number of times directed

[ ] - Complete work specified in brackets the number of times directed

" - inches

PUFFY BABY HAT

MATERIALS:

-Crochet Hook Size H

-Yarn Needle

-Yarn Of Your Choice

INSTRUCTIONS:

-Stitches: ch, dc, sc, sc ps, sl st.

-Sc Ps (Single Crochet Puff Stitch)

-Round 1: Ch4, 11dc in the 4th ch from the crochet hook. Join with a sl st in top of beginning ch4. (12dc)

-Round 2: Ch1, but do not turn the work. 2sc between all sts. (24 sc) Join with a sl st in the first sc.

-Round 3: Ch1, and then turn the work. Sc in same st. Scps in next st. (Sc in the next st. Scps in the next st) around. Join with a sl st in the first sc. (12sc & 12scps)

-Round 4: Ch1, and turn the work. 2sc in each st. Join together with sl st in the first sc. (48sc)

-Round 5: Rep R3. Pay attention that your scps properly (24sc & 24scps)

-Round 6: Ch1, and turn the work. Sc in each st. (48sc)

-Alternate Round 3 and Round 6 until you've made 10 rounds of scps, and end with Round 3.

-Tie off.

WRIST BAG

MATERIALS:

-Lion Brand Chenille (Thick & Quick)

-Hook Size J

-Two 3" Craft Rings or Bamboo Rings

INSTRUCTIONS:

-Stitches: ch, sc, sl st, hdc.

-Row 1: Ch 15, hdc in the 3rd ch from crochet hook. Hdc in each of the remaining ch.

-Rows 2-7: Ch2, turn the work. Hdc in each st.

-Row 8: Ch1, turn. Work over the craft ring as you advance, sc in each st on row 7.

-Tie Off.

HOW TO JOIN:

-Start on row 6. Hold both pieces of the work together. Now you will join the pieces with a sl st in each corresponding sts on row 6.

-Sc in each corresponding sts around to the exact same location on the opposite side, placing 3 scs in each of the corners on the bottom.

-Tie Off.

ADDITIONAL EMBELLISHMENTS:

-Add beautiful lining of fabric to the inside of the purse.

-Celebrate at holiday parties with a bag made from your favorite holiday colors.

-Add a little sparkle and pizzazz with ribbons, rhinestone, pearls, gems, etc.

Printed in Great Britain
by Amazon

44133219R00057